D1537317

THE CENTRAL DIVISION

BY ROBERT E. SCHNAKENBERG

Published in the United States of America by
The Child's World® • PO Box 326
Chanhassen, MN 55317-0326

800-599-READ • www.childsworld.com

ACKNOWLEDGEMENTS

The Child's World®: Mary Berendes,
Publishing Director

Editorial Directions, Inc.: E. Russell Primm, Editorial
Director and Line Editor; Katie Marsico, Managing
Editor; Caroline Wood, Editorial Assistant; Susan
Hindman, Copy Editor; John Barrett, Proofreader;
Tim Griffin, Indexer; Kevin Cunningham, Fact
Checker; James Buckley Jr. and Jim Gigliotti,
Photo Reseachers and Photo Selectors

Manuscript consulting and photo research by
Shoreline Publishing Group LLC.

The Design Lab: Kathleen Petelinsek,
Design and Page Production

Photos:
AP: 8
Brian Bahr/Getty: 27
Andrew D. Bernstein/NBAE/Getty: 24
Bettmann/Corbis: 9, 21, 22, 23, 35, 37
Duane Burleson/AP: 1
Nathanial S. Butler/NBAE/Getty: 15, 30
Darron Cummings/AP: 33
Tony Dejak/AP: 16
Jesse D. Garrabrant/NBAE/Getty: 12, 41
Frank Gunn/AP: 19
Jeff Haynes/AFP/Getty: 10, 29
Andy Hayt/NBAE/Getty: 26
Tom Hood/AP: 13
Ron Hoskins/NBAE/Getty: 5, 34
Rusty Kennedy/AP: 38
Wilfredo Lee/AP: 4
Fernando Medino/NBAE/Getty: 18
Jeff Roberson/AP: 2
Chuck Robinson/AP: 32
Jack Smith/AP: 7
Sports Gallery: 36
Mark Terrill/AP: Cover
Elaine Thompson/AP: 40
Jamie-Andrea Yanak/AP: 20

**LIBRARY OF CONGRESS
CATALOGING-IN-PUBLICATION DATA**
Schnakenberg, Robert.
  The Central Division / by Robert Schnakenberg.
    p. cm. — (Above the rim)
  Includes index.
  ISBN 1-59296-526-1 (library bound : alk. paper)
  1. National Basketball Association—History—Juvenile
literature. 2. Basketball—West (U.S.)—History—
Juvenile literature. I. Title. II. Series.
  GV885.515.N37S35 2006
  796.323'640973—dc22   2005024777

TABLE OF CONTENTS

INTRODUCTION

The Central Division of the National Basketball Association (NBA) got a new look in the 2004–05 season, but it was home to an old story: some great basketball played by some of the biggest stars in the game.

The division was born in the 1970–71 season, when the league first expanded to four divisions and 17 teams. At the time, it didn't

**The Pistons won the revamped Central Division in
2004–05 and advanced to the NBA Finals.**

The Pacers and Bulls each reached the NBA playoffs in 2004–05.

look anything like the current version. That season, the division included the Atlanta Hawks, Cincinnati Royals (who are now the Sacramento Kings), the Cleveland Cavaliers (who were in their first season), and the Baltimore Bullets (who are now the Washington Wizards). The Cavaliers are the lone holdovers still in the group.

After a couple of seasons, Houston moved in and Cincinnati moved out. The division went through lots more changes over the next couple of decades and eventually grew to eight teams: the Hawks, Chicago Bulls, the Cavaliers, Detroit Pistons, Indiana Pacers, Milwaukee Bucks, New Orleans Hornets, and Toronto Raptors. When the NBA went through another major **realignment** before the 2004–05 season, the Bulls, Cavaliers, Pistons, Pacers, and Bucks remained in the Central.

One thing has stayed consistent, though: the Central Division has been home to some fantastic basketball. The Pistons won 54 regular-season games in 2004–05 to win the division crown, then advanced all the way to the seventh and deciding game of the NBA Finals before their bid for a second consecutive league title was stopped by the San Antonio Spurs.

In all, current Central teams have accounted for 10 NBA championships. And over the years, the division has featured some of the game's legendary players, such as Michael Jordan, Elvin Hayes, and Nate Archibald. Current stars such as LeBron James are building on this tradition of excellence. Read on to learn about this exciting division's past—and future.

Team	Year Founded	Home Arena	Year Arena Opened	Team Colors
Chicago Bulls	1966	United Center	1994	Red, white, and black
Cleveland Cavaliers	1970	Gund Arena	1994	Wine and gold
Detroit Pistons	1941	The Palace of Auburn Hills	1988	Red, white, and blue
Indiana Pacers	1967	Conseco Fieldhouse	1999	Blue and gold
Milwaukee Bucks	1968	Bradley Center	1988	Green, purple, and silver

CHAPTER ONE

THE CHICAGO BULLS

**Finals MVP Michael Jordan and coach Phil Jackson hoist
trophies after the Bulls won the 1998 championship.**

When people think of the Chicago Bulls, they immediately think of Michael Jordan. But while "Air Jordan" is the most important figure in Bulls history, he's not the only one. The Bulls have been entertaining fans in the Windy City for nearly four decades.

The Bulls' dance team, which entertains the home crowd throughout the games, boasts one of the NBA's most inventive nicknames: the Luvabulls.

The Bulls began play in 1966. The new squad quickly won the city over by posting the best record ever for an **expansion** team, 33–48. It was even good enough to make the **playoffs,** where the Bulls were eliminated by the St. Louis Hawks.

The Bulls did not build on that early success until the 1970s, however. That's when a new group of players led by Bob Love and Norm Van Lier led the team to four straight 50-win seasons and a regular spot in the NBA playoffs. Defensive specialist Jerry Sloan, one of the original expansion Bulls, was also a standout in this period. His

Bob Love was the Bulls' most prolific scorer—until Michael Jordan, that is.

Guard Norm Van Lier helped usher in a period of success in the 1970s.

hard-nosed play helped Chicago capture a division title in 1975.

Injuries and the retirement of key players ended the Bulls' competitive run, however. The team slid into a long period of mediocrity. That began to end

Former Bulls center Luc Longley was the first Australian to play in the NBA.

Scottie Pippen (No. 33) and Michael Jordan were a formidable duo in the Windy City.

when Michael Jordan joined the team in 1984. The athletic guard out of the University of North Carolina made an immediate impact on the franchise. He won the NBA Rookie of the Year award and emerged as one of the NBA's top scorers. But Jordan's high-flying dunks weren't enough to make the Bulls a contender. The team had to add other good players around him.

Important **role players** such as Scottie Pippen and Horace Grant helped Chicago capture the Central Division crown in 1991. The Bulls capped that season by defeating the Lakers in five games to win Chicago's first NBA title. Additional championships followed in 1992, 1993, 1996, 1997, and 1998. Long considered a laughing-stock, the Bulls became the standard by which other teams measured themselves.

Individually, Jordan joined the ranks of the all-time greats. In 1986–87, he led the league in scoring for the first of seven consecutive seasons—and 10 times in all—by averaging 37.1 points per game. One year later, he won the first of his five league MVP awards. And he was named the Finals MVP each of the six seasons that the Bulls won the championship. In 15 NBA seasons in all, Jordan averaged 30.1 points per game, the highest figure in league history.

Jordan was much more than a scorer, though. He also was a superb defensive player who was an All-NBA defensive first team choice nine times and was named the league's defensive player of the year in 1988. He had an indomitable will to win, too, and helped make everyone around him a better player.

Jordan's retirement in 1998 (he eventually came back to play

Guard Chris Duhon, a rookie in 2004–05, was one of several youngsters who helped the Bulls make the playoffs.

While playing for Orlando in 1990, Bulls head coach Scott Skiles amassed a league-record 30 assists in a game against Denver.

two seasons for the Washington Wizards) ended one of the most successful runs of any team in sports history. After he left town, the Bulls struggled to develop a new identity as a team.

Phil Jackson, the man who coached Chicago to each of its NBA titles, left at the same time as Jordan, and the Bulls went through a series of head coaches while trying to rekindle their winning ways. They missed the playoffs six consecutive seasons before breaking through under former NBA guard Scott Skiles in 2004–05. That year, Chicago won 47 regular-season games—its most since Jordan's last season—finished second in the Central Division, and reached the **postseason.**

Center Eddy Curry led a balanced attack by averaging 16.1 points per game, while young guards Kirk Hinrich, Ben Gordon, and Chris Duhon gave fans of "Da Bulls" lots to cheer about.

Guard Ben Gordon is a star on the rise in Chicago.

The Cleveland Cavaliers seem to specialize in heartbreaking defeats. Like Major League baseball's Chicago Cubs, they climb out from the bottom of the standings every few years, only to tumble back down again once they get close to success. If nothing else, these ups and downs have made them interesting to watch.

The Cavaliers joined the NBA in 1970. It was not a promising beginning. The team went 15–67 and played in a half-empty arena. About the only thing the team had going for it was coach Bill Fitch's sense of humor. "I phoned Dial-a-Prayer," Fitch said during one bad losing streak, "but when they found out who it was, they hung up."

It took a long time, but Cleveland's prayers were finally answered. Led by center Nate Thurmond, the team enjoyed its first winning season in 1975–76. The Cavaliers captured the Central Division title and made it all the way to the Eastern Conference Finals. There Fitch and his crew suffered the first of many heartbreaks, falling to the Boston Celtics in six games.

The Cavaliers' home court, Gund Arena, is the only one in the NBA named after a team owner—business-man Gordon Gund.

From 1978 to 1987, Cleveland fielded consis-tently poor teams, never winning more games than it lost. Things began to improve in the late 1980s. The team drafted talented young players like Brad Daugherty, Ron Harper, and Mark Price. No matter

Brad Daugherty is the leading scorer and rebounder in the Cavaliers' history.

how good the team got, however, it could not seem to get past the Chicago Bulls, led by Michael Jordan. In 1989, Jordan's **jumper** at the buzzer sent an excellent Cavs squad home early from the playoffs. A few years later, in 1993, he did it again. The Cavs also fell to the Bulls in the 1992 Eastern Conference Finals.

The team's name was chosen by the fans as part of a newspaper contest. A cavalier is a soldier mounted on a horse.

LeBron James' arrival in 2003 helped transform the Cavaliers.

After these shatter-
ing defeats, the Cavaliers
began the long process
of **rebuilding.** They used
the draft and signed
foreign-born players
such as center Zydrunas
Ilgauskas in an attempt
to return to playoff contention. The
biggest news in Cleveland in a decade,
though, came when the Cavs drafted
LeBron James in 2003.

Only 18 at the time, the multi-
talented James quickly became one of
the NBA's best, and most popular, players. He was named the league's rookie of
the year in 2003–04, when he averaged
20.9 points, 5.5 rebounds, and 5.9 assists
per game. Only two NBA rookies before
him averaged more than 20 points,
5 rebounds, and 5 assists per game:
all-time greats Oscar Robertson and
Michael Jordan.

James immediately made the
Cavaliers a better team, too, help-
ing them win 35 games (after only 17
the previous season). Unfortunately, it

In 2003, the Cava-
liers announced a
return to the team's
original uniform col-
ors—wine and gold.
They had switched
to orange and blue
in 1983.

Center Zydrunas Ilgauskas was an All-Star in the 2004–05 season.

In LeBron James' first season in Cleveland in 2003–04, the Cavaliers averaged 18,288 fans per game—a big increase over the 11,497 mark of the previous year.

soon meant more heartbreak for Cavaliers' fans. In 2004–05, the club appeared poised to reach the playoffs for the first time in seven seasons until streaking New Jersey edged Cleveland for the final Eastern Conference spot.

Still, the Cavaliers went 42-40, posting a winning record for the first time since 1997–98. James averaged 27.2 points per game and emerged as

"King James" already is one of the NBA's marquee players.

General manager Danny Ferry (left) and new coach Mike Brown (right) have
surrounded LeBron James with a capable supporting cast.

In March 2005,
LeBron James
became the young-
est player in NBA
history to score 50
points in a game.
He scored 56 points
at Toronto just 80
days after his 20th
birthday.

one of the NBA's most recognizable stars. Ilgauskas
chipped in with 16.9 points and 8.6 rebounds per
game and made the All-Star team.

After the season, former Indiana Pacers assistant Mike Brown was hired as head coach, and the
Cavaliers signed versatile guard Larry Hughes and
veteran forward Donyell Marshall to help give "King
James" a talented supporting cast. They hope to soon
turn heartbreak into joy in Cleveland.

CHAPTER THREE

THE DETROIT PISTONS

One of the NBA's oldest franchises, the Detroit Pistons never won a championship until the arrival of Isiah Thomas and his "Bad Boys" of the late 1980s. After a rebuilding period in the 1990s, the team recently has returned to glory.

The Pistons were founded in 1941 by an automobile piston maker named Fred Zollner. He based

One of the key players on the Pistons' championship teams was Vinny "Microwave" Johnson—so named because he could "heat up" quickly.

The Pistons played in Fort Wayne, Indiana, until 1957.

his team in Fort Wayne, Indiana, and called it the
Fort Wayne Zollner Pistons. After several years in the
NBL, the club joined the NBA's Central Division in
1949. They made the NBA Finals in 1955 and 1956,
losing both times. The Pistons then fell on hard times,
becoming one of the NBA's worst teams.

Relocated to Detroit, Michigan, in 1957, the
Pistons cracked the .500 mark only three times from
1957 through 1983. Their best years came in the

Talented guard Dave Bing starred for the Pistons in the 1970s.

**Center Bob Lanier's inside game complemented
Dave Bing's outside game for the Pistons.**

mid-1970s, when they were led by the talented inside-
outside tandem of guard Dave Bing and center Bob
Lanier. In 1980, the franchise bottomed out, winning
only 16 of 82 games. The only good thing about the
Pistons' poor play was that it allowed the team to
get high draft picks. The team used these to draft the

The NBA Western
Conference cham-
pionship trophy is
named in honor
of Pistons founder
Fred Zollner.

**The Pistons beat the Bulls in the Eastern Conference
finals in 1989 en route to the NBA title.**

backcourt duo of Isiah Thomas and Joe Dumars. Detroit also traded wisely, picking up **big man** Bill Laimbeer and other important role players.

In 1989, all this wheeling and dealing paid off. The Pistons won 63 games—a franchise record—and the team's first-ever NBA title. Led by coach Chuck Daly, the club employed a bruising defense that earned it the nickname Bad Boys. The "Bad Boys" were even badder in 1990, stomping the Portland Trail Blazers in five to win a second consecutive championship.

After these glory years, age caught up with some of the Pistons' best players. The franchise regained a great deal of its energy in the 1990s with the arrival of Grant Hill, a dynamic forward out of Duke University. In 2001–02, the retooled Pistons surprised many NBA observers by winning 50 games and capturing the Central Division title. To do so, they employed a defensive style that reminded longtime fans of the champions of the past.

Detroit won 50 games again and repeated as division champs the next year, then rose to the top of the NBA in 2003–04. That season, Hall of

> In one stretch of the 2003–04 season, the Pistons held five consecutive opponents to fewer than 76 points. That's an NBA record.

Detroit easily handled the favored Lakers in the 2004 NBA Finals to win its third league championship.

Fame coach Larry Brown took the helm, and the Pistons went 54–28 during the regular season.

Veteran forward Rasheed Wallace was a key midseason acquisition, joining players such as Ben Wallace, Richard Hamilton, Chauncey Billups, and young Tayshaun Prince. Though the roster did not feature superstars, the players blended together as a formidable team. In the Finals, the Pistons were heavy underdogs to the Lakers, but won easily in five games.

Detroit set out to repeat as champs in 2004–05—and almost did it. The Pistons won 54 games again and took the Central crown for the third time in four seasons. They reached the NBA Finals again before losing to the San Antonio Spurs in a thrilling seven-game series.

Despite the narrow defeat, the Pistons clearly are back in the driver's seat in the Motor City.

Tayshaun Prince is one of many pieces in the Pistons' team-oriented puzzle.

CHAPTER FOUR

THE INDIANA PACERS

> **The Pacers were named after the pace car used in the running of the hometown Indianapolis 500.**

Basketball is big in Indiana. The Hoosier State's passionate fans have rooted hard for their hometown Pacers since 1967. They have witnessed some terrific basketball, and they have come "this close" to seeing their team win an NBA championship.

From 1967 to 1976, the Pacers played in the old American Basketball Association (ABA). The league was known for its freewheeling style of play and the use of red-white-and-blue basketballs. The Pacers won the ABA title three times and drew large and enthusiastic crowds. When the ABA merged with the NBA in 1976, the popular Pacers were invited to join the enlarged league.

At first, Indiana struggled in the NBA. In their first 13 seasons, they posted only one winning record. Fans still came out to cheer them on, however. Billy Knight and George McGinnis were a couple of the stars of that period. The Pacers joined the NBA's Central Division in 1979.

In the late 1980s, the Pacers' fortunes improved. The team added sharpshooting forward Chuck Person, who was known as "the Rifleman," and a talented center from Holland, Rik Smits. Holland is a county in the country of the Netherlands. The team's most important young player, though, was guard Reggie Miller from University

Dutchman Rik Smits was a towering force, both rebounding and scoring.

of California, Los Angeles (UCLA). He became one of the league's best **clutch shooters.** With this **nucleus** of players, the Pacers stormed into playoff contention. In 1994, 1995, and 1998, the team made it all the way to the Eastern Conference Finals. Though they lost all

Former Pacer forward Wayman Tisdale is now a successful jazz guitarist.

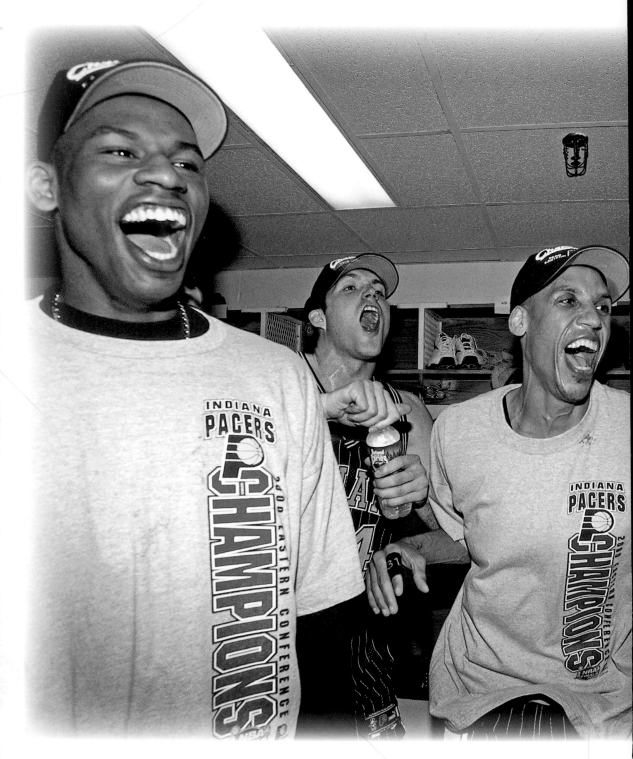

The Pacers were all smiles after winning the conference championship in 2000.

three times, Miller's
heart-stopping last-
second shots excited
Pacer fans and made
them feel an NBA
title was just around
the corner. The team
even hired Indiana
basketball legend Larry Bird as coach
in 1997 to make that dream a reality.

In 2000, the Pacers finally got
their big chance. The team faced
the Los Angeles Lakers in the NBA
Finals. The Lakers, led by Shaquille
O'Neal, were heavily favored. But
the tough-minded Pacers would
not go down easy. They fought
the Lakers in a tough six-game
series before losing the final game,
116–111.

It was a difficult loss to take.
Some critics said the Pacers were too
old to compete again for an NBA
title. However, the club immediately
began rebuilding for the future.
Bird, the former Boston Celtics' star,
gave way to another Hall of Famer,

**The Pacers' home
arena, Conseco
Fieldhouse, was
designed to look
and feel like a high
school gymnasium.**

Head coach Larry Bird and star guard Reggie Miller carried the Pacers to the brink of an NBA title.

Larry Bird, the Pacers' president of basketball operations, was a college star at Indiana State.

former Detroit Pistons' guard Isiah Thomas, as coach, but eventually became the club president. Forwards Jermaine O'Neal and Ron Artest joined Miller in 2000–01, and the club still made the playoffs even though it dropped to fourth place in the Central Division.

Jermaine O'Neal has blossomed into a top scorer for the Pacers.

Reggie Miller got a standing ovation after leaving the
final game of his career in 2005.

Reggie Miller made
at least 100 three-
point field goals for
an NBA-record 15
consecutive seasons
from 1989–1990
through 2003–04
(he had 98 the
season before
the streak started
and 96 the year it
ended).

After that, it was a steady climb back to the
top, capped by a club-record 61 regular-season
wins under new coach Rick Carlisle in 2003–04. The
division-rival Pistons ended Indiana's league title
hopes in the conference finals that season and in the
conference semifinals the next year. Miller retired
following the 2004–05 season after a brilliant 18-
year career in which he became only the 13th player
in league history to amass more than 25,000 points
(25,279).

CHAPTER FIVE

THE MILWAUKEE BUCKS

**The Bucks, who beat the Lakers in this playoff series in 1971, won a league
championship faster than any other expansion franchise in sports.**

The Milwaukee Bucks got off to a record-breaking start. They
won a league championship in just their third season in
1970–71—faster than any other team in sports history. While there
have been some lean years since then, for the most part the Bucks
have been consistent winners since they joined the NBA in 1968.

Bucks legend Kareem Abdul-Jabbar appeared in the 1980 comedy movie *Airplane!* as copilot Roger Murdock.

The Bucks can thank a lucky coin toss for their early success. In 1969, the team won the toss to determine who picked first in the NBA draft. Milwakee selected UCLA center Lew Alcindor, who would later change his name to Kareem Abdul-Jabbar. He led the Bucks to the conference title in his rookie season. The next year, the graceful big man helped Milwaukee

Kareem Abdul-Jabbar, originally known as Lew Alcindor, was the league MVP three times in his six seasons in Milwaukee.

Oscar Robertson, the man they called the "Big O,"
was one of the best all-around players ever.

win the NBA title. He spent six seasons in Milwaukee and was named the NBA's Most Valuable Player in 1971, 1972, and 1974.

The other star player with the Bucks at this time was Oscar Robertson. Nicknamed "the Big O," Robertson was a veteran **point guard** who excelled at making tough passes. The teamwork between these two future Hall of Famers made the early 1970s a golden era for Bucks basketball.

In November of 1977, the Bucks trailed the Hawks by 29 points with less than nine minutes to play. But Milwaukee outscored Atlanta 35-4 the rest of the way to win the game 117–115.

High-flying Glenn Robinson was an All-Star, but he
couldn't lead the Bucks to new heights.

After Robertson retired and Abdul-Jabbar moved on to the Los Angeles Lakers, the Bucks struggled. They did not win 50 games in a season again until 1981. They won the Central Division that year and the next five years in a row. In fact, the Bucks enjoyed 12 straight winning seasons from 1979–1980 through 1990–91. But the team never could make it back to the NBA Finals.

In the 1990s, the Bucks went into a period of decline. Many thought the arrival of forward Glenn "Big Dog" Robinson in 1994–95 would reverse their fortunes, but it did not happen immediately. The club did not return to the top of the Central Division until 2001. That year, head coach George Karl's team won 52 regular-season games, then advanced to the conference finals before taking Philadelphia to seven games. Robinson averaged 22.0 points per game and got lots of help from players such as guards Ray Allen and Sam Cassell.

Things haven't gone smoothly in the ensuing years. Milwaukee hasn't won a postseason series since then, and the club slumped to last place in the Central Division in 2004–05. After the season,

Milwaukee's Michael Redd set an NBA record for three-pointers in a quarter when he sank eight of them in the final period of a game against the Rockets in 2002.

**Guard Michael Redd averaged a team-leading 23.0 points
per game for Milwaukee in 2004–05.**

The Bucks hope that center Andrew Bogut will become an NBA star.

head coach Terry Porter was let go, and replaced by Terry Stotts.

The Bucks did get a stroke of good fortune after the season, however. Though they had just a 6.3 percent chance of drawing the top pick in the NBA draft lottery, they got lucky again and came out with the number-one choice. Milwaukee fans hope that the "luck of the Bucks" that helped them become so good so quickly soon will turn things around again!

With the top overall selection in the 2005 draft, the Bucks chose Andrew Bogut of the University of Utah.

TIME LINE

1941   The Pistons are founded as the Fort Wayne Zollner Pistons

1966   The Chicago Bulls are founded

1967   The Indiana Pacers begin play in the ABA

1968   The Milwaukee Bucks are founded

1970   The Cleveland Cavaliers are founded

1971   Milwaukee wins its first—and to date, only—NBA title

1976   The Indiana Pacers join the NBA

1989   The Detroit Pistons win the first of their back-to-back NBA titles

1991   Chicago wins the NBA title for the first time, and the first of three years in a row

1998   Michael Jordan wins his fifth league MVP award, and the Bulls win their sixth championship

2004   Detroit beats Los Angeles in five games in the NBA Finals to win the league championship

STAT STUFF

TEAM RECORDS

TEAM	ALL-TIME RECORD	NBA TITLES (MOST RECENT)	NUMBER OF TIMES IN PLAYOFFS	TOP COACH (WINS)
Chicago	1,613–1,552	6 (1997–98)	25	Phil Jackson (545)
Cleveland	1,249–1,589	0	13	Lenny Wilkens (316)
Detroit	2,185–2,297	3 (2003-04)	36	Chuck Daly (467)
Indiana	*1,586–1,504	0	*26	Bob Leonard (*529)
Milwaukee	1,616–1,386	1 (1970–71)	24	Don Nelson (540)

*includes ABA

NBA CENTRAL CAREER LEADERS (THROUGH 2004–05)

TEAM	CATEGORY	NAME (YEARS WITH TEAM)	TOTAL
Chicago	Points	Michael Jordan (1984–1993, 1994–1998)	29,277
	Rebounds	Michael Jordan (1984–1993, 1994–1998)	5,836
Cleveland	Points	Brad Daugherty (1986–1996)	10,389
	Rebounds	Brad Daugherty (1986–1996)	5,227
Detroit	Points	Isiah Thomas (1981–1994)	18,822
	Rebounds	Bill Laimbeer (1981–1994)	9,430
Indiana	Points	Reggie Miller (1987–2005)	25,279
	Rebounds	Mel Daniels (1968–1974)	7,643
Milwaukee	Points	Kareem Abdul-Jabbar (1969–1975)	14,211
	Rebounds	Kareem Abdul-Jabbar (1969–1975)	7,161

MORE STAT STUFF

MEMBERS OF THE NAISMITH MEMORIAL NATIONAL BASKETBALL HALL OF FAME

CHICAGO PLAYER	POSITION	DATE INDUCTED
George Gervin	Guard	1996
Robert Parish	Center	2003
Nate Thurmond	Center	1985

CLEVELAND PLAYER	POSITION	DATE INDUCTED
Chuck Daly	Coach	1994
Walt "Clyde" Frazier	Guard	1987
Nate Thurmond	Center	1985
Lenny Wilkens	Guard/Coach	1989

DETROIT PLAYER	POSITION	DATE INDUCTED
Walt Bellamy	Center	1993
Dave Bing	Guard	1990
Larry Brown	Coach	2002
Chuck Daly	Coach	1994
Dave DeBusschere	Forward	1983
Harry "the Horse" Gallatin	Forward	1991
Bob Houbregs	Forward/Center	1987
Bailey Howell	Forward	1997
Harry "Buddy" Jeannette	Guard	1994
Bob Lanier	Center	1992
Earl Lloyd	Forward	2003
Bob McAdoo	Forward	2000
Bobby McDermott	Guard	1988
Dick McGuire	Guard	1993
Andy Phillip	Guard	1961
Isiah Thomas	Guard	2000
George Yardley	Forward	1996
Fred Zollner	Owner	1999

MORE STAT STUFF

MEMBERS OF THE NAISMITH MEMORIAL NATIONAL
BASKETBALL HALL OF FAME

INDIANA PLAYER	POSITION	DATE INDUCTED
Larry Brown	Coach	2002
Alex English	Forward	1997
Jack Ramsay	Coach	1992

MILWAUKEE PLAYER	POSITION	DATE INDUCTED
Kareem Abdul-Jabbar	Center	1995
Nate "Tiny" Archibald	Guard	1991
Dave Cowens	Center	1991
Alex English	Forward	1997
Bob Lanier	Center	1992
Moses Malone	Center	2001
Oscar Robertson	Guard	1980

GLOSSARY

backcourt—in this instance, a term for the guards in a team's lineup; it also refers to the area on a basketball court from the centerline to the baseline that a team defends

big man—another term for center

clutch shooters—players who are skilled at making especially long or difficult shots

expansion—enlarging the league to admit new teams; expansion teams often struggle in their first few seasons

jumper—a shot in which a player jumps into the air and releases the ball from above his head; also called a jump shot

nucleus—the core group of players around which a team is built

playoffs—a four-level postseason elimination tournament involving eight teams for each conference; levels include two rounds of divisional playoffs, a conference championship round, and the NBA Finals (all series are best-of-seven games)

point guard—the player who brings the ball upcourt for the offensive team

postseason—another name for the playoffs; a team must make it through three rounds to reach the NBA Finals

realignment— a change in the way something is organized

rebuilding—the process of building a team back up again after a period of poor play

role players—players who specialize in one or two aspects of the game, such as defense or rebounding

FOR MORE INFORMATION ABOUT
THE CENTRAL DIVISION AND THE NBA

BOOKS

Aretha, David. *The Detroit Pistons Basketball Team.* Berkeley Heights, N.J.: Enslow Publishers, 2001.

Firsh, Aaron. *The History of the Detroit Pistons.* Mankato, Minn.: Creative Education, 2002.

Firsh, Aaron. *The History of the Indiana Pacers.* Mankato, Minn.: Creative Education, 2002.

Hareas, John. *Basketball.* New York: DK Publishers, 2005.

Miller, Raymond H. *Michael Jordan.* San Diego. Kidhaven Press, 2003.

Nichols, John. *The History of the Chicago Bulls.* Mankato, Minn.: Creative Education, 2002.

Nichols, John. *The History of the Cleveland Cavaliers.* Mankato, Minn.: Creative Education, 2002.

Nichols, John. *The History of the Milwaukee Bucks.* Mankato, Minn.: Creative Education, 2002.

Stewart, Mark. *LeBron James.* Chicago: Raintree, 2005.

Stewart, Mark. *The NBA Finals.* New York: Franklin Watts, 2003.

ON THE WEB

Visit our home page for lots of links
about the Central Division teams:
http://www.childsworld.com/links

Note to Parents, Teachers, and Librarians: We routinely verify our Web links to make sure they are safe, active sites—so encourage your readers to check them out!

INDEX

ABOUT THE AUTHOR

Robert E. Schnakenberg has written eight books on sports for young readers, including *Teammates: John Stockton and Karl Malone* and *Scottie Pippen: Reluctant Superstar*. He lives in Brooklyn, New York.